Landscape painting, at the end of the 20th century, finds itself in a strange case, one that is at once highly topical and critically peripheral. Even within the last year or so, for example, we have seen significant art-historical study made of the emergence, at the turn of the 16th into the 17th century, of landscape painting as an autonomous genre. Last year we had 'The Landscape of Rubens', at the National Gallery, and currently at Antwerp (coming to the British Museum in the autumn) is a study of Van Dyck among his contemporaries as a founder of the European 'plein-air' tradition of the landscape water-colour study. To take us on into the 18th and early 19th centuries, at this very moment, again at the National Gallery, we have in the delightful loan exhibition of the Gere Collection of small landscape paintings, a celebration of the 'plein-air' painting 'sur le motif' as practised in every European school. And of course there is the more general point that in The Landscape we pride ourselves in particular in our very own, peculiarly English contribution to European art. In the work of those heroes, Turner and Constable, to say nothing of Gainsborough, Girtin, Cox, Palmer, Linnell and all the rest of them, we celebrate what many would argue as the very greatest of English painting.

A hundred years ago, the situation was perhaps even more extreme, with landscape painting at large at the radical tip of the modernist adventure, from Monet and Pissarro to Van Gogh and Cezanne. But how different it is now. At home or abroad, can we think of a landscape painter as such, pure and simple, whom any country could seriously think of as a worthy representative at, shall we say, the Venice Biennale, without making itself a laughing stock? Diebenkorn for America in the late 1970s, Auerbach for Britain in the mid-1980s and Kossoff four years ago are the only ones of any standing that I can think of, and to cite them is only to reinforce the point. For with none of them was landscape of itself the point. All of them had another justification, a special plea, a modernist programme.

The paradox is that with so much else that now fills the Biennale every time - conceptual art, video and installation - the subject-matter can quite happily be summoned up in aid. Just as the particular response to landscape was once the principle justification in terms of the politically-correct 'issue' that it happens to address. Today fashionably Green 'issues', or ecological pessimism, agricultural or organic intervention, may be all very well, but the landscape as something to sit in, and look at, and try to make sense of in formal terms? - you must be joking. Is there a single young landscape painter who, these days, could realistically be nominated for the Turner Prize, or bought for the Arts Council's collection, or sent on a British Council tour, or win a scholarship to the British School at Rome? Of course not, for the simple truth is that Landscape painting is

David Hockney

Hotel Acatlan: Two Weeks Later 1995
Diptych lithograph printed in colours
From the Moving Focus series
Edition 98
73 x 188 cms
Courtesy: Berkeley Square Gallery

off the critical and curatorial agenda, and has been for some considerable time, perhaps since Victor Pasmore went abstract just after the War.

And yet, and yet... As was always bound to be the case, there is still a very great deal of landscape being done, and not by any means all unworthy of serious consideration. The Royal Academy summer show is full of it, the Small South Room notoriously so, and the conventional wisdom is that most of it is rubbish. Yet by its modest engagement and unselfconscious competence, it stands naturally in that honourable tradition of 'plein-air' painting, looking to Cezanne perhaps, and his 'petit sensation', but also back further and more generally, to Corot, Sisley, Constable, Wilson and Thomas Jones. To look at landscape more closely, as I sometimes do, is of course, in these ungenerous times, to put

the onus very much upon personal judgement, but any unprejudiced and fair conclusion can only be that rather a lot of modern landscape is good. Landscape represents, in fact, the serious continuation of that long-established tradition of looking, understanding and response, in the open air before the subject, that was once, albeit a long life-time ago, as serious a thing as a painter could do. And to forget of ignore this, or to persuade oneself that it hardly matters now, is to mask a fundamental truth.

For we have only to look at the history of art to know that nothing is immutable. Times change, the world moves on and comes around again. And while through the period of modernism, we cannot but recognise the significance of the avant-garde as an idea, and the actual achievement of successive avant-gardes in practice, we must also recognise the fact that modernism is a

6 August –
19 September
1999

CONTEMPORARY BRITISH LANDSCAPE

Flowers East

William Crozier

Garden 1999
Oil on canvas
198 x 213.5 cms

comparatively new idea. Certainly there is nothing in the rules to say that it must now last for ever. If post-modernism means anything, it can only mean that the period of successive avant-gardes, each following close upon the heels of each, has run its course, and that the narrow imperatives of any current avant-garde orthodoxy have been replaced by something broader, more open, concurrent, simultaneous. This is not to say that most interesting and important things may not be done on the conceptual or manifestly experimental fringes of this vast spectrum of opportunity and activity, but the concommitant possibility is no less clear: that the truest and most radical of contemporary art may be done by an artist sitting in a field, like Van Gogh or Cezanne, and painting the view.

It is most useful, therefore, that from time to time there should be exhibitions such as this which, far from taking a particular position, or following a narrow programme, rather take the broader, more open and generous view. The point is not that work of a certain kind is for the moment the only acceptable sort, or another kind of work irrelevant. Rather it is that in embracing both the radical and the apparently conventional approach, all that matters is that the work should be good, honest and true to itself.

William Packer *July 1999*

Leon Kossoff
Christchurch No.1 1987
Charcoal and pastel on paper
76 x 56 cms
Courtesy: Annely Juda Fine Art

Jock McFadyen

3 Colts Lane 1998
Oil on canvas
192 x 380 cms

Humphrey Ocean

William Blake   1991-94
Oil on canvas
132.5 x 244.4 cms

Boyd & Evans

Ubehebe 1999
Oil on canvas
91 x 183 cms

John Wonnacott

The Barclays Building & St Pauls from
Tower 3 of the Lloyds Building 1992-95
Oil on board
104.1 x 133.3 cms
Courtesy: Agnews

Don McCullin

Scotland 1996
Silver gelatin print
Open edition
40.5 x 51 cms
Courtesy: Hamiltons Gallery

Roger Palmer

Gare Loch 1996
Silver gelatin print
Edition 3
94 x 121 cms

Tai-Shan Schierenberg

Norfolk Landscape 1999
Oil on canvas
76.5 x 76.5 cms

John Kirby

The River 1999
Oil on canvas
101 x 76 cms

Elizabeth Magill

Way Out West 1996
Oil on canvas
15 x 18 cms

Peter Howson

Landscape with Lighthouse 1999
Oil on canvas
92 x 122.5 cms

Lucian Freud

Garden in Winter   1998-99
Etching on somerset paper
Edition 46
94 x 60 cms
Courtesy: Timothy Taylor Gallery

Norman Ackroyd

Coniston Water (Ruskins House) 1998
Monotype and watercolour on Japanese paper
61 x 44.5 cms

Prunella Clough

Grass Plot   1998
Oil on canvas
81 x 53.5 cms
Courtesy: Annely Juda Fine Art

George Rowlett

From Deal to Ramsgate 1998
Oil on board
61 x 183 cms
Courtesy: Art Space Gallery

Jiro Osuga

Untitled (Blackbird in a Tree) 1999
Oil and acrylic on canvas
224 x 81.5 cms

Ben Whitehouse

Hampstead Heath 1999
Oil on canvas
170 x 244 cms
Courtesy: Belloc Lowndes Fine Art

Ann Dowker

Western Aspect from Prini Ropa   1996
Oil on canvas
122 x 183 cms

Peter Archer

Towards Another Evening (Going Home) 1998-99
Oil on canvas
147.5 x 188 cms
Courtesy: Austin Desmond Fine Art

Beverley Daniels

Black Mountain   1998
Oil on canvas
44 x 28.5 cms

John Hubbard

Sea Wrack   1993
Oil on canvas
152 x 193 cms

Julian Cooper

Kirkstone Boulder 1993-94
Oil on canvas
137 x 213.5 cms

David Hepher

From Peckham to Athos 1998
Acrylic, bituminous, spray paint, photographic
vinyl and concrete on canvas
235 x 305 cms

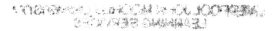

Steve Pyke

Landscape   1981-98
Silver gelatin prints
61 x 76.2 cms

Andy Goldsworthy

Red Stone Sea, Heysham Head   1992
Photograph
89 x 81 cms
Courtesy: Michael Hue-Williams Fine Art

Kenneth Draper

Dark Walls 1991
Pastel on paper
51 x 46 cms
Courtesy: Hart Gallery

Jean Macalpine

Intersect 1998
Hand toned photograph
46 x 57 cms
Courtesy: Hart Gallery

Patrick Hughes

The Perspective Hinge 1999
Oil on board
82.5 x 175 x 19 cms

Dick Lee

Back Garden, Ingleville
Oil on canvas
180 x 152 cms

Brendan Neiland

Glencoe 1995
Screenprint
Edition 100
61 x 43.3 cms
Courtesy: Redfern Gallery

Jeffery Camp

Puddles on the Cliff 1987
Oil on canvas
45.5 x 51 cms
Courtesy: Browse & Darby

Adrian Berg

Leighton Hall, 14th July 1991
Oil on canvas
134 x 205.5 cms
Courtesy: Piccadilly Gallery

John Loker

Hot Scene 1998
Mixed media on canvas
107 x 132.5 cms

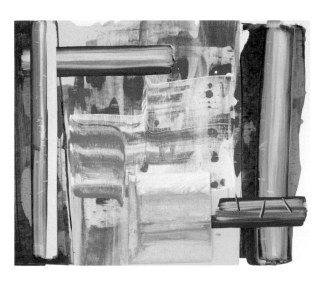

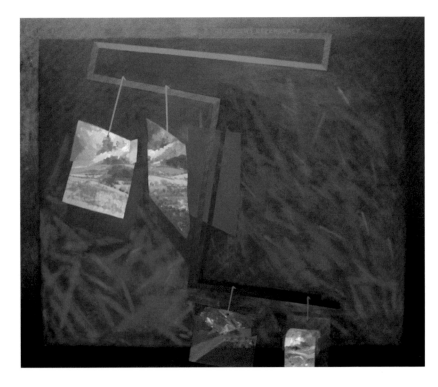

David Leverett

A Precarious Dependency 1999
Oil on canvas
152.5 x 182 cms

John Davies

Abandoned Mine Shafts, Tynewydd 1993
Silver gelatin print
Edition 5
50 x 60 cms
Courtesy: Zelda Cheatle Gallery

Josef Herman

Landscape near Hundon 1956-57
Oil on canvas
46 x 61 cms

Renny Tait

Lighthouse with Landscape 1999
Oil on canvas
91.5 x 91.5 cms

Frank Auerbach

Park Village East 1998
Oil on board
50.8 x 55.9 cms
Courtesy: Marlborough Fine Art

Tom Phillips

Landscape in La Mancha:
Return of the Knight 1999
Mud on paper
50.5 x 40.5 cms

Roger Mayne

Snow Pattern, North Iceland 1993
Silver gelatin print
30 x 40 cms
Courtesy: Zelda Cheatle Gallery

Jane Joseph

The Thames at Kew Bridge 1999
Charcoal and chalk
85 x 114 cms

Derek Hirst

Winter Was Hard No.II 1992
Cryla on panel
102 x 127 cms

Lucy Jones

Outside 1999
Oil on canvas
214 x 305 cms

Peter Prendergast

Approaching Storm 1996
Acrylic on paper
80 x 129 cms
Courtesy: Boundary Gallery

Christopher Le Brun

The Shell Gate 1980
Oil on canvas
248 x 139 cms
Courtesy: Marlborough Fine Art

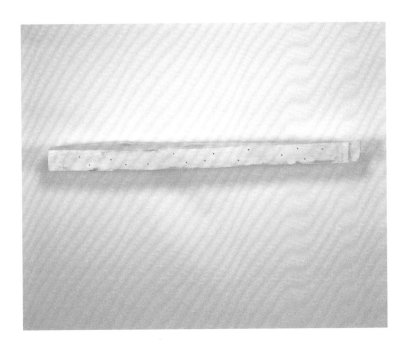

Ainslie Yule

Offshore 1999
Wood, gesso and wax
8 x 126 x 16.5 cms

Carole Hodgson

horizontal II 1999
Cellulose fibre with iron filler
124 x 99 x 14 cms

John Virtue

Landscape No. 365 1997-98
Black ink, shellac and acrylic on canvas
305 x 610 cms
Courtesy: Michael Hue-Williams Fine Art

Ray Atkins

Goonvean Pit – Winter 1996
Oil on board
183 x 183 cms
Courtesy: Art Space Gallery

Gwen O'Dowd

Uaimh 30 1998
Mixed media on canvas on board
122 x 168 cms

Terry Setch

Into the Picture 1999
Mixed media
264 x 240 cms

Panel 1: The Watchers
Panel 2: The Exodus
Panel 3: Windsurfing

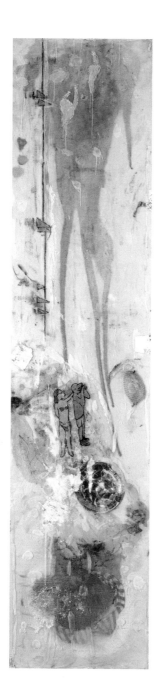

Fay Godwin

Large white cloud near Bilsington 1981
(from The Saxon Shore Way Series)
Silver gelatin print
40 x 30 cms
Courtesy: Zelda Cheatle Gallery